Coaching & Scouting

CAREERS
OFF THE FIELD

MC

Coaching & Scouting

By James Buckley Jr.

Mason Crest

450 Parkway Drive, Suite D
Broomall, PA 19008
www.masoncrest.com

Printed and bound in the United States of America.

Series ISBN: 978-1-4222-3264-4
Hardback ISBN: 978-1-4222-3267-5
EBook ISBN: 978-1-4222-8525-1

First printing
1 3 5 7 9 8 6 4 2

Produced by Shoreline Publishing Group LLC
Santa Barbara, California
Editorial Director: James Buckley Jr.
Designer: Bill Madrid
Production: Sandy Gordon
www.shorelinepublishing.com
Cover photo: Dreamstime.com/Monkey Business Images

Library of Congress Cataloging-in-Publication Data is on file with the publisher.

CONTENTS

Key Icons to Look For

Words to Understand: These words with their easy-to-understand definitions will increase the reader's understanding of the text, while building vocabulary skills.

Sidebars: This boxed material within the main text allows readers to build knowledge, gain insights, explore possibilities, and broaden their perspectives by weaving together additional information to provide realistic and holistic perspectives.

Research Projects: Readers are pointed toward areas of further inquiry connected to each chapter. Suggestions are provided for projects that encourage deeper research and analysis.

Text-Dependent Questions: These questions send the reader back to the text for more careful attention to the evidence presented here.

Series Glossary of Key Terms: This back-of-the-book glossary contains terminology used throughout this series. Words found here increase the reader's ability to read and comprehend higher-level books and articles in this field.

Foreword
By Al Ferrer

So you want to work in sports? Good luck! You've taken a great first step by picking up this volume of CAREERS OFF THE FIELD. I've been around sports professionally—on and off the field, in the front office, and in the classroom—for more than 35 years. My students have gone on to work in all the major sports leagues and for university athletic programs. They've become agents, writers, coaches, and broadcasters. They were just where you are now, and the lessons they learned can help you succeed.

One of the most important things to remember when looking for a job in sports is that being a sports fan is not enough. If you get an interview with a team, and your first sentence is "I'm your biggest fan," that's a kiss of death. They don't want fans, they want pros. Show your experience, show what you know, show how you can contribute.

Another big no-no is to say, "I'll do anything." That makes you a non-professional or a wanna-be. You have to do the research and find out what area is best for your personality and your skills. This book series will be a vital tool for you to do that research, to find out what areas in sports are out there, what kind of people work in them, and where you would best fit in.

That leads to my third point: Know yourself. Look carefully at your interests and skills. You need to understand what you're good at and how you like to work. If you get energy from being around people, then you don't want to be in a room with a computer because you'll go nuts. You want to be in the action, around people, so you might look at sales or marketing or media relations or being an agent. If you're more comfortable being by yourself, then you look at analysis, research, perhaps the numbers side of scouting or recruiting. You have to know yourself.

You also have to manage your expectations. There is a lot of money in sports, but unless you are a star athlete, you probably won't be making much in your early years.

I'm not trying to be negative, but I want to be realistic. I've loved every minute of my life in sports. If you have a passion for sports and you can bring professionalism and quality work—and you understand your expectations—you can have a great career. Just like the athletes we admire, though, you have to prepare, you have to work hard, and you have to never, ever quit.

Series consultant Al Ferrer founded the sports management program at the University of California, Santa Barbara, after an award-winning career as a Division I baseball coach. Along with his work as a professor, Ferrer is an advisor to pro and college teams, athletes, and sports businesses.

Introduction

Like any other coach, Bill Pintard is a juggler. It's game day, and his Santa Barbara Foresters college summer-ball baseball team will be taking on its archrival, the Conejo Oaks. First pitch is hours away, but Pintard is already hard at work. Before he gets home tonight, he'll juggle a dozen different tasks, even though his job title is simply, "Coach." As this book will show, coaching is about much more than just the time on the field. Coaches at every level need to be experts at the game they teach. They need to understand strategy, game and roster management, and the rules of the game. They have to be leaders, and able to organize and inspire people—often young people—to do their best and work together for the common goal of winning.

Being a successful coach also means being successful at a wide range of skills. It's not enough just to have a whistle, a clipboard, and a loud voice. Coaching today is a complex job with many moving parts. (Note: We'll touch on scouting a bit later in this introduction.)

Game Day Morning

It's a rough morning already. Pintard has a bit of a cold, his team lost last night, and there is a problem at home he'll have to deal with later. He's having a bad day. However, he knows that he can't take that feeling to the ballpark.

"To be a successful coach, you cannot have a bad day," says Pintard, who has led his team to five National Baseball Congress World Series championships since 2006 and has won more than 800 games as the Foresters' manager. "Or if you are having a bad day, you have to hide it. If you verbalize that you're having a bad day, then it's okay for your assistant coaches and your players to have a bad day. As a leader, you can never have bad days."

So, no matter how he is feeling, he puts on his game face and heads out.

Before heading to the ballpark, Pintard is on the phone ordering equipment. The team is running short on baseballs and, at this level of the sport, there's no one else to make sure the Foresters have this vital piece of the baseball puzzle. He's got dozens of emails to return. Some are from players who want to join the team. It's early in their summer season, so he has his eye out for additions that can help fill roster spots. Assembling and organizing the roster is perhaps the coach's most important **administrative** function. A coach will typically work harder and longer at the office or doing paperwork than he or she does on the field.

A coach is pulled in many directions on game day. Pintard takes a moment to answer a few questions from a local reporter.

A Foresters' **intern** calls, and Pintard has another issue to deal with. The concession-stand operator is having trouble getting ice delivered. Isn't that for someone at the ballpark to handle? Normally the answer is yes, but just about anything will end up on a coach's desk. It's all about being flexible.

Next up: finances. Pintard's team has to raise all the money it needs to support its 50-game summer season. At a high school, a coach might meet with booster clubs or attend a bake sale to help raise extra money that the team does not get from the school system. A college coach will connect with team sponsors, such as companies that advertise in the stadium. Even in the pros, a coach or manager will need to spend time meeting with people and companies whose money makes the whole system run.

For Pintard, the community is the main source of the team's support. He talks with a bank president for about 15 minutes, filling her in on the team's chances this summer and describing the ways that the bank's name will appear on tickets and a banner at the ballpark.

Pintard has been working as a coach for more than two hours today, and he has yet to set foot on the grass infield.

Running the Clubhouse

Once his office work is done, Pintard can finally head to the ballpark. That's when his work really gets going. Even as he walks in from the parking lot, he is met by the intern about the ice situation; thanks to a little muscle, the ice is in place for the game. That's one problem solved.

A reporter comes up and needs "a couple minutes, Coach," to tape an interview for the radio. Pintard tells him he'll be free once he checks in with his other coaches. A fan of the team, at the ballpark early to watch batting practice, stops by to shake Pintard's hand. He has an idea about who to pitch against Conejo. Pintard listens politely, and moves on as soon as he can. Fans are part of the bargain of just about any sports situation. Learning to understand and deal with them takes patience and practice.

He still has not reached his office before a player corners him to make sure that Pintard knows the player's mom will be at the game. The reason for letting Pintard know? The player wants to make sure he gets in the game today, so his mom can watch him play. It's a 19-year-old college sophomore asking, but everyone wants to make their mom happy.

Finally, Pintard reaches his office, where the members of his coaching staff are waiting. After greeting them all, he settles into his desk chair for a short meeting on the roster and the game. The coaches go over strategy against Conejo, as well as the lineup they'll put on the field. The coaches pass along any news about players, including injuries or other things that might affect Pintard's decisions.

Putting on a team windbreaker, Pintard finally heads to the field, where his team is warming up. Warm-ups take about two hours, during which time Pintard also visits with the opposing coach, deals with the radio interview, and meets more fans.

Finally, after meeting with the umpires and standing with the team for the national anthem, Pintard watches his team take the field. After more than five hours of work on game day, he is finally ready to do what he actually does: coach the team during the game.

After more than four hours at the ballpark, Coach Pintard (19) finally joins his team on the field.

Scouting for the Future

If Pintard's schedule seems busy already, add to that the fact that he is also wearing another hat. He is a scout for the New York Yankees, charged with looking for young players who might be worthy of being asked to join a pro team. He's not the only scout at the game, either. A half-dozen men stand behind home plate with radar guns. They each work for a separate Major League Baseball organization. Like scouts in every sport, they are using their knowledge of the game, their understanding of physical movement, and their experience to try to predict the future. A scout sees a young player but has to imagine that same player in three, five, or even ten years. Will he mature into a pro? Will the raw skill he has now translate to refined skill later? What are the needs of the team the scout works for? Does the team need a particular position filled?

Pintard watches both teams for players with the spark to be worth following more closely. After this game, he'll write reports on some of those players and try to see them again to gain more information. On days that the Foresters are not playing, he'll attend other games, traveling several hours if needed, to try to find that next superstar.

Coaches and scouts have chosen to spend their life around sports. They get the excitement of competition and the occasional joy of winning. From high school to the Super Bowl, though, they will all tell you: It's not a game. It's hard work.

Words to Understand

empathy: an ability to understand and feel compassion for another person's point of view or emotions

Getting Started

CHAPTER 1

People with a goal to coach a sport at any level above youth leagues have a path to take. Often that path starts with their time in a uniform on the field of play. Nearly all coaches have played their sport at some level. It's not necessary, but the examples of coaches who never played their sport are few and far between.

With the experience of playing the game as the most likely first step, the next step is to look inside to see if they have what it takes to coach. Wanting to stay in the game and keep winning is a great start, but it takes much more than that. Just like the work the person did in making the team as a player, he or she will have to start all over again to make the grade as a coach, working their way up the ladder. More than ever before, becoming a coach is an involved process, but a person with the right makeup and a strong work ethic can make that goal a reality.

It Starts With Passion

As we'll see, coaching is not normally a job in which a person can make a whole lot of money. There is money to be made at the top of the pyramid, certainly in the pros or at a major college, but those are just a tiny fraction of the thousands of coaching positions available. The majority of coaching jobs are in high school and college, not the pros. Those jobs don't pay pro-level salaries, so something else has to draw a person in.

Tim Vom Steeg played college and pro soccer, and became a teacher and coach. He led the University of California at Santa Barbara (UCSB) men's team to the 2006 NCAA championship after coaching the Santa Barbara City College team to a state title. He's been with UCSB since 1998.

"I'm a competitive person," he says. "I have enjoyed competing since my college days as a player. I like the idea that we can bring a group of guys together and see if we can beat everybody we play. If you're thinking that playing is over, you have to ask if you're still fired up to win games."

Pam Tanase has coached water polo and swimming and diving at the club, high school, and collegiate levels. She looks away from the pool for some of the benefits she gets from coaching.

"I love it," she says. "You don't do this for the money. You get to work with people who have a common interest. You want to see the kids succeed, not just in sports, but in life. I think sports can teach you a lot of things that are true in any part of life, and it's great to be a part of that teaching process. You have to have a passion for that if you want to be in coaching."

Indeed, having that kind of commitment and passion for the sport will help you with every other part of your job as a coach. You won't be able to lead people unless you totally believe in yourself and your sport first.

Other Skills

"First of all, they have to be great communicators," says Eric Flannery, who has led his St. Edward High School team to a pair of Ohio state basketball championships. He also works with the U.S. National Under-17 Team. "You have to be able to talk to different types of people in different ways. I think any coach also has to be someone who has a lot of **empathy,** who can understand what other people are going through. You have to understand when people are having good days or bad days. You need to keep an open line of communication all the time, in both directions— listening to them or talking to them."

Along with talking to other people, you have to be able to organize yourself. Time management skills are vital to a coach. The Foresters' Bill Pintard has a famous saying about helping players learn to manage their schedules: "You're either on time or you're late. There is no 'early.'" For the coach, that means being more on time than the players. It also means knowing how to organize practice schedules and travel times, how to let players recover from games, and how to juggle—there's that word again—the responsibilities of the job.

Beyond time management, coaches need administrative skills. Paperwork is part of the job, whether filling out contracts, ordering supplies, or writing up reports. It might seem as if sports people don't do a lot of writing, but a coach needs to be able to write well and quickly, as well as manage his and others' time.

Education for a Coach

Passion, communication skills, and time management, however, are not enough anymore. Being a great game manager or an inspiring leader is not enough, either. At nearly every level other than professional coaching, a good record in school is vital.

"Anyone who wants to be a coach today absolutely has to think about getting a college degree," says Justin Aspegren, a pitching coach for Santa Barbara (Calif.) City College and a former summer-ball manager. "Outside of pro players who come back to coach, a college degree is something any aspiring coach has to have these days. I would even say that a master's degree or some graduate background will really help in finding a job."

Indeed, many high school coaches do double duty as classroom teachers. They need to have earned their degrees before they can get a job in a school system. For such people, coaching is just part of their long days on campus. Having a degree, especially a master's, is great as a fallback, too, several coaches pointed out. Coaching is not the most stable job in the world, and a few bad seasons can send a coach out of the sports world. Without a college degree, a job outside sports might be very hard to find.

"If you want to be in college coaching, you need to work as a G.A. [graduate assistant] during and after your time in college," Flannery suggests. "If you are aiming at a high school job, you'll need to get degrees and certifications to become teachers. There are not too many jobs in high school for coaches who are not also teachers."

Potential coaches might see a teammate from high school make the jump to the pros in baseball or even basketball or sign up for a big scholarship in football. However, anyone aiming at coaching can't stop their education after high school.

Scouting Skill Set

For the related field of scouting, most experts say that an education is not as important, but that other skills are invaluable.

Gary Woods spent ten seasons in the major leagues as an outfielder. After his playing career, be became an area scout for the Chicago White Sox, responsible for a large part of central and southern California. Woods laid out the key skills for a scout.

"Number one, you have to be a self-starter, and you have to be organized," he said. "You have to be a very good time manager. You have limited days to see these players. For instance, Division I starting pitchers might only have fourteen starts in a season, and only half of them will be at home games that you can see. You have to plan ahead to make sure you see all the ones you want to see. And you have to be buttoned-up enough to know that your supervisors can get to see them, too."

Baseball scouts use radar guns to gauge the speed of pitches thrown by players they are evaluating.

A scout needs to see this high school pitcher and project what this young man will become.

Robby Massar, a young scout for the New York Yankees and a former college baseball player, agrees. "To be a scout, you have to be self-driven," he says. "You don't have a boss sitting next to you. There's no one in the office watching you. You have to be accountable."

Woods also said that a big appeal for him in scouting is that he can maintain the kind of competitive drive that helped him succeed in the majors. "Everyone is out there looking for that one star no one else has found. It's a thrill to be the one that makes that find."

Finally, Woods noted that scouts have to be able to see beyond what your eyes are telling you.

"You also have to have good instincts for people," he said. "Part of this job is measuring the visual observable—arm strength, speed, hitting power, etcetera—but you have to look past that. Can you measure attitude, drive, coachability, disposition…things that you can't figure out with a stopwatch or video?"

Scouts working in baseball, basketball, or football, or even people looking to discover the next great young tennis players or golfers, all have that in common. They are looking at a young person and they need to visualize that person in the future.

While a team sports coach needs to be a juggler, a scout for any sport needs a crystal ball.

Text-Dependent Questions

1. What does Coach Flannery suggest as a good place to start building coaching experience?

2. What level of education should a high school coach aim for?

3. Name one important trait for a pro scout.

Research Project

Find a youth sports league in your area and contact them about the steps needed to become a volunteer coach or assistant coach. Also, ask your school if such coaching would count toward community-service hours.

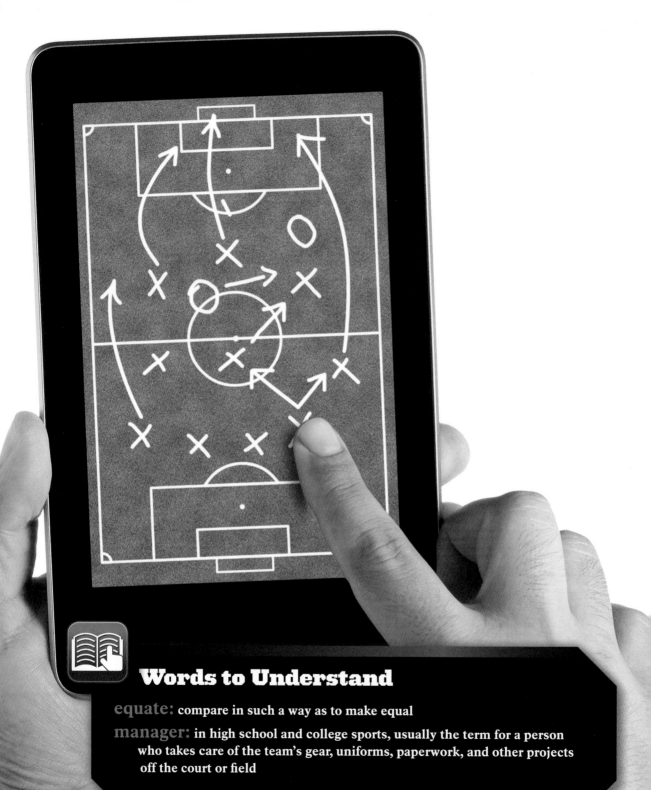

Hard at Work

People want to get into coaching because they love the Xs and Os. That is, they relish the thought of showing other people how to play the games they love. They want to choose the players, make up the game plans, and inspire athletes to succeed. They want to win. However, as any coach will tell you, getting to the moment of winning takes a lot of hard work . . . most of it far from the field of play.

High School Coaching

High school coaches are teachers first, part-time parents second, and coaches third. Young athletes in high school need a lot more from their coaches than simply tips on playing. High school coaches are involved in many areas of their student-athletes' lives. They'll provide nutrition advice, help with finding the right teachers, or even talk with them about the dangers of illegal drugs.

Coaching a high school sport combines mentoring with teaching the athletic skills needed.

Part of the job is making students understand their job as role models for younger students and as representatives of the entire school.

Working as a coach in high school means working with young minds as with bodies. For every superstar athlete who will go on to fame and fortune, there are dozens who might never play again after high school.

Greg Malling is the head coach of the football program at Wisconsin's Arrowhead High School. He told *Coach and Athletic Director* magazine, "One thing we always talk about is making sure you are creating hope for a lot of athletes. Some players are going to get two or three plays a game, but they're great young men, so having those plays is a great reward for them. It's not just championships, but how we are building better people."

Justin Aspegren from Santa Barbara City College adds to that sentiment, "That's the A-number-one most important part of coaching—the teaching part. It's more than just winning. It's helping young people realize their potential. I get more out of seeing the underachiever improve than I do out of helping the star stay on top."

High school coaches in any sport also have to understand what their teenage players are going through in their lives, as their bodies and emotions grow and change.

"They don't want to be different, they want to fit in, they're shy," says Bill Pintard of the Santa Barbara Foresters. "You can't make fun of them. You have to understand that they have fragile self-esteem. If you have to criticize a player during practice, you have to make sure to see them afterward to tell them that it's okay and they have to move on."

A high school coach walks the line between teacher and coach; the successful high school coach has probably mastered both of those skill sets.

College Coaching

For coaches as well as student-athletes, college is the next step up the ladder. The athletes continue to have—or are supposed to have—an equal focus on academics. At a Division I school, a coach will often demand a higher level of time and energy from the athletes than a coach will at lower-division or smaller schools.

Along with choosing the team, organizing practices, and running the games, college coaches in most sports have an additional job: recruiting. They need to convince top high school athletes to choose their schools. It can be a daunting, time-consuming, and frustrating task. Tim Vom Steeg knows that all too well. He has been the head men's soccer coach at the University of California at

Volunteer First

Along with getting their education, future coaches need to show they can do the job. Whether aiming for high school, college, or pro coaching, one of the best ways to do this, and learn along the way, is to work for free: volunteer.

"I have four guys on my current staff, full-time employed teachers, who used to be volunteer managers for my basketball team," says Flannery. "If someone realizes that they won't make the team, we tell them there are ways to stay involved with the game. One of those ways is to be a volunteer coach, help with youth or rec programs, or stay with your high school as a trainer or manager. I tell people who love the game to stay involved any way you can and learn from as many people as you can."

Santa Barbara since 1999. A two-time NCAA Coach of the Year, he led his team to the 2006 NCAA championship, as well as seven Big West Conference titles. Yet each year, he starts the process of finding players again.

"In a way, it's the most important part of the job if you're going to enjoy success," he says. "Even a moderately bad coach with a talented team will be successful. There isn't a lot of conversation about recruiting skills, but if you're not able to attract kids, then it'll be very difficult for a [college] coach to enjoy success."

Vom Steeg and other coaches follow extensive rules laid out by the NCAA while doing their recruiting. They take annual

Coaches like UCSB soccer's Tim Vom Steeg have mastered coaching on and off the field.

Star high school basketball player John Houston was one of thousands of athletes who chose their colleges after a long recruiting process.

tests to make sure they know those rules. Breaking them can draw severe punishments to the school or the coach's program. Even with the rules

designed to level the playing field, some coaches are simply better at this than others.

"The recruiting part is two parts," Vom Steeg explains. "One is the athlete who is attracted to the coaches themselves. They want to play for that coach, feel like that coach will make them a better player or person. The second is players who are attracted to the program or to the university. Certain coaches who have both going on are the ones that win most of the championships."

Pam Tanase had to recruit young women for her college water polo teams. That sport offers little in the way of scholarship money, so she had to use other methods. "I **equate** recruiting to a sale," she says. "You have to be persuasive and you have to get to know the person you're recruiting, in order to know what they want above and beyond the athletics. You can sell them on your school and what it can provide for them beyond the sport. It takes a lot of time, on the phone, and now texting. And in some sports, you've got home visits with parents, too."

For college coaches, add to all that recruiting time a busy schedule of meeting with sponsors, or "boosters," that help pay for the school's program. Then toss in a larger amount of media work, especially at the highest levels, and most college coaches have left the classroom behind long ago.

Pro Coaching

The vast majority of coaches at the professional level in the major sports have had long playing careers, either in college or at various levels from minors to the top leagues.

Mickey Kelleher spent 11 seasons in the major leagues as an infielder. After he put away his glove, he spent another 22 years as a coach with several teams. In 2009, he was the first-base coach for the World Series champion New York Yankees. "To be honest, it's really difficult to get job in professional coaching if you have not been a pro player," he says.

For those who do climb that ladder, however, there are new challenges to face when moving from teammate to coach. Kelleher spoke about how he

Former infielder Mickey Kelleher is one of hundreds of players who successfully made the transition to coaching.

had to adapt when he moved from the field to the bench…and face another kind of competition.

Even at the professional level, coaches are called on to be teachers, leaders, and organizers.

"It was hard for the first couple of years, getting over the fact that you were not playing anymore," he says. "Physically, I thought I could still play. I did have the communications and teaching skills, though, and was able to do that job. Getting the job was the same process of going through the competition to advance. There are a lot of people who want these jobs."

Scouting for Pro Teams

While coaches can find jobs at many levels of sports, scouts work almost exclusively for pro teams (though some talent evaluators can work for sports agents). Pro scouts have a difficult job, searching through thousands of pounds of coal looking for one shining diamond.

"There can be very long days," said White Sox scout Gary Woods. "Here's a typical Friday during the season. I'm up at five A.M., get breakfast, and work out. Then I check my schedule and do some reports. Then I'm in the car and might drive to see a high school game in Thousand Oaks at two or three o'clock. Then I go to an afternoon game at Pepperdine University. Then down to a night game at UCLA, and then get home at midnight. The next morning, I might have the same thing again, but with even more games."

Yankees scout Robby Massar, who is just starting out his scouting career, added: "The biggest thing from my perspective as a younger scout is to always have your ears open; don't think you have all the answers. There is always

The best moment for a scout comes when a young person signs a deal to join the organization, in this case scout Gary Woods of the White Sox.

more to learn. Be a sponge, especially when you're around these guys who have been doing this for decades in some cases."

Scouts need experience to truly succeed. That can take a long time to build up, but starting out they all faced the same challenge: long days on the road, looking for gold.

Text-Dependent Questions

1. Name two things that high school coaches might have to advise their athletes on beside sports.

2. Other than teaching athletes, what is the other key job for college coaches?

3. What is one difference between a pro coach and a college coach?

Research Project

Pick your favorite pro team and read an online biography of the head coach and some of the top assistants. Find out what road they took to reach their jobs. How many played in the pros? How many just played in college? What other jobs have they had?

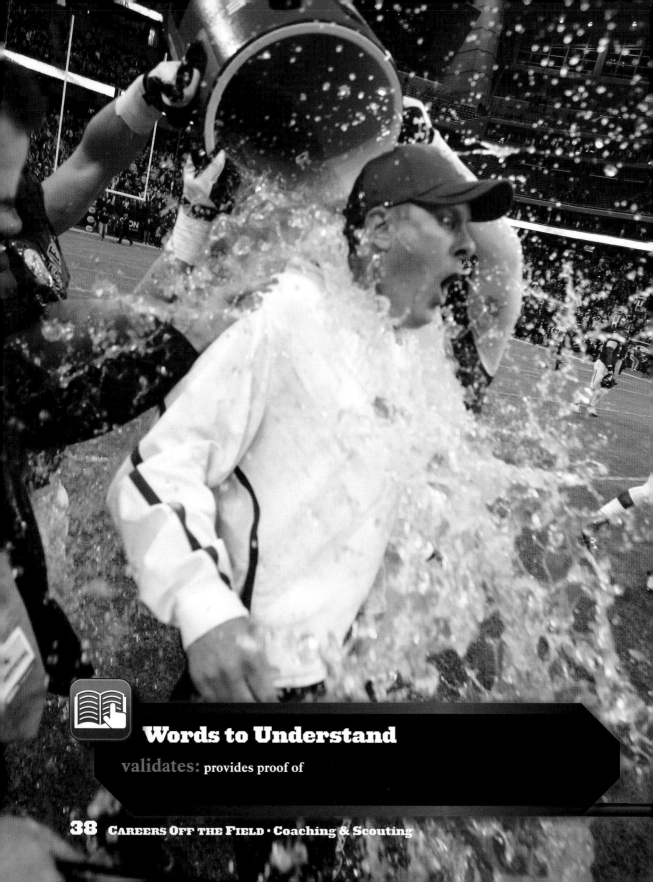

Words to Understand

validates: provides proof of

Realities of the Workplace

CHAPTER 3

Coaching might look like a pretty nice job. You get to go to all the games, of course, and if you do well, you might see your name in the paper. You get to be in charge and tell people what to do. You get to wear the uniform again, if you're in baseball, or you get lots of great gear, if you're in college. In high school, you can relive the joy that you experienced in your own high school career. If you make it all the way to the professional ranks, the monetary reward can be great.

However, as with any job, coaching has some downsides, too. Not everyone makes it to the top, and not everyone gets to coach a winner. It's only fair that future coaches understand that while there can be the occasional Gatorade shower (there's an example shown at left), there are also a lot more hard, long, low-paying days along the way.

Smaller college sports such as lacrosse cannot pay their coaches as much as big sports can.

You're Not Going to Get Rich

The level at which coaches work determines their level of pay. A high school coach doing part-time duty after working all day as a teacher might get an extra few thousand dollars a year. In some places, it can be even less. College coaches in a "minor" sport such as water polo or volleyball can probably make a living, but they will also probably need to take on extra work in their off-season to really get by. Coaches in the lower levels of pro sports, such as in minor league basketball or baseball, might only get paid during their seasons, which can be as short as five months. At the higher levels, of course, in the NFL or the NBA, coaches make millions. However, just as only an incredibly tiny few of the millions of high school athletes ever make it as millionaire pro players, that's true of coaching, too. It's a hard road to "winning the lottery," as CAREERS OFF THE FIELD advisor Al Ferrer says.

"The majority of coaches are not going to make a lot of money," agrees basketball coach Eric Flannery of St. Edward High School in Ohio. "You're getting into this for the love of the sport. But you need to understand that from

Although a successful high school coach, Eric Flannery adds to his calendar by working with U.S. national teams.

the beginning. You can make a living and support a family, but you have to prepare for that. It can be manageable, depending on you and your family."

Lots and Lots of Time

Whether part-time or full-time, coaching can take a lot of hours during the season in which the sport is active. Along with multiple games per week, there are practices and the time to travel from place to place. Even in high school, there can be hours-long bus rides in some large, rural districts. Once the games are over, there is paperwork and communications work that adds to the coach's workload. All that time can take a real toll on a person.

"Sometimes, I think it can be psychologically overwhelming," says Santa Barbara City College baseball coach Justin Aspegren. "I do what I can to make it work for me and my family. But mentally, it can be hard. You put so much of your time and focus on the coaching. When a game is over, there's nothing you can do about it, but it's easy to take it home with you. I think that's where a lot of people lose that balance. It takes a special personality to be able to shut that down and leave it at the ballpark or the stadium. Having a really good support system at home, a wife or husband who understands your passion, helps."

Coaches such as Justin Aspegren learn to combine their passion for the game with their family responsibilities.

Burnout is a regular issue at lower levels of coaching.

"There are young, energetic coaches willing to do whatever they can to get into a school system," athletic director Kevin Flegner of Wisconsin's Arrowhead High School told *Coach and Athletic Director* magazine. "But after a few years, they get married and find out what the time commitment really is. They realize they can make more money teaching other courses."

At higher levels, it can be even more involved. Many NFL coaches have comfortable couches installed in their offices, making it easier to simply sleep there instead of spending time going home. Weeks with 80 or 90 hours of work are not uncommon during the season for college football or basketball coaches, too.

In Major League Baseball, the long season combines with many long road trips to turn spring and summer into a life lived out of a suitcase. The time commitment for any sports coach is huge, and one that has to be managed well to make for a successful coaching life.

Losing Is Hard

Every coach at every level—high school, college, or pro—has to deal with one of two outcomes for every contest. The team wins or the team loses. The winning is always great. The losing can be very hard. The coaches' job, though, is not to focus on the score, but to find

Club Coaching

Many sports now have another layer of competition at the high school level. Sports such as soccer, volleyball, baseball, and lacrosse have private club teams. Those teams hire coaches separately from high schools. Typically, these coaches are experienced and can bring a higher level of instruction than just a volunteer could. If you have experience at a high level, such as working with high school or college teams or many years at a high youth level, clubs might be an option. Note that many clubs call for coaches to be certified by national organizations. Getting those licenses involves classroom and field work, as well as passing tests. Look into clubs in your area and find out how they are organized.

the positives in the performance.

"You can play up to your potential, have a good process, and lose," says Bill Pintard of the Santa Barbara Foresters. "That doesn't mean everything you're doing is wrong. If you're executing and playing well, some days you just get beat. The other

Losing is a part of sports. By accepting it gracefully, coaches lead by example for their players.

team might have a really good pitcher that day, or you lose on some fluke play.

"Not every win is the same, not every loss is the same," he continues. "You need to take the right lessons from each case. You can win and still be upset with how you played or with the effort. You can lose and find something positive. The key is to focus on the development of the players and if they are doing

Coach Pintard congratulates his team on another W at the ballpark.

what you expect them to with the process you've communicated. They can exceed your expectations, but they're never going to exceed their ability. You have to understand what they can do… their best is good enough."

That doesn't mean that in private the coach can't express disappointment to his family or to his assistant coaches. With the players, the coach has to maintain the right attitude. Getting down or angry after a loss allows the players to act the same way.

Encouraging and looking for the positive gives players another way to deal with their frustrations.

Finally...Winning

The flip side of losing, of course, is winning. For many who want to be coaches, that is the best part of the job. You get the satisfaction of completing a task and of overcoming obstacles. You don't do the work on the field, of course. That's up to your players. The glory of those moments of winning is, for many coaches, the payoff for the many hours of other work that is not quite as glamorous or glorious.

"Well, I'm certainly a competitor and want to win," says Flannery. "Being in the arena and competing is a big part of this. But the biggest thrill I get is when a player comes back after they graduate and tells me how special the time we had together was and what they learned here. There's not a better feeling in the world than hearing that. When they tell you that you had a big impact on their life, no matter what they did, that gives me my biggest thrill. The relationships you build are way more important than winning."

Pintard adds, "Winning **validates** effort on the practice field, but it does that for you, too, since there's a lot of time that goes into your practice plans. When you win, it shows you that the process that you're using is working. It also validates the time and effort of the players."

Even at the pro level, the winning is what drives much of the passion. "Winning as a player was the greatest experience," says Mickey Kelleher, who played for five major-league teams and coached for three clubs. "As a coach, winning was very satisfying, too. The feeling is the same, the greatest feeling in the world. Just because we didn't play didn't stop us from jumping up and down and pouring champagne."

Winning is the end result of the hard work, organization, and thoughtful effort by coaches and players working together.

Scouting: Hard Road

Coaching has some drawbacks, and so does scouting. Scouts get to do what they love: watch their favorite sport day after day. As Gary Woods noted, though, the amount of time is daunting.

There is also Woods' warning: "Scouting jobs are really, really hard to come by. You can want it all you want, but so many of these jobs go to people who played [professionally] and have good reputations, and a lot go to family members in baseball. There's a lot of people who get jobs through those connections.

So it's not a career that, even if you set your mind to it, you can have a one-hundred percent chance of achieving."

Don't stop trying and working toward a goal of being a coach or a scout, but make sure you understand the realities of what might lie ahead.

Women in Coaching

The vast majority of coaches at every level of sports are men. Nearly all women who are coaches are coaching female athletes. There are some exceptions, of course. In 2014, the NBA's San Antonio Spurs made Becky Hammon the first female assistant coach in any of the major pro sports. Some women are assistants at the college men's level. However, if you are a young woman wanting to get into coaching, chances are very high that your best chances are with women's sports.

When women do get into the coaching arena, they face some challenges that men may not, including how they ar perceived by others. "When our male coach yells at the officials, the response is different than if our female coach yells," says Pam Tanase, a longtime coach in water polo and swimming and diving. "You also have to be ready to be the only female coach in the room. There might be a committee

Coach Pam Tanase films her dive team in action. She and other experts counsel female coaches to have a strong sense of self.

or league meeting, and you might be the only woman."

The advice from Tanase and other top female coaches is to look within for the answer. "You need a strong sense of self and a strong coaching philosophy," Tanase says. "That helps when you encounter different people who want you to go another way, and you can have principles to stick to. Having strong principles is really important."

That sense of self can be vital when facing a very tough job market. The University of Minnesota reports that in 1974, soon after the passage of Title IX that created laws calling for equal numbers of sports for both men and women in college, 90 percent of women's sports were coached by women. In 2014, that number had dipped to 40 percent. The number of such jobs are fewer and now more and more of them are going to male coaches. Becoming a coach is a hard job. Becoming a coach when you're a woman is even harder.

Male or female, being a coach calls for a wide range of personal and professional skills. The experts in this book are united in two opinions: They love their jobs…and what they do is hard work, not just fun in the sun.

Text-Dependent Questions

1. What do coaches say about how much money one can make in this profession?

2. What does athletic director Kevin Flegner say causes some young coaches to change jobs?

3. How can a loss help a team?

Research Project

Find a job posting for a coaching position at a high school or college near you. What is the school looking for? What skills and education does it request? How would you fill out an application for such a job?

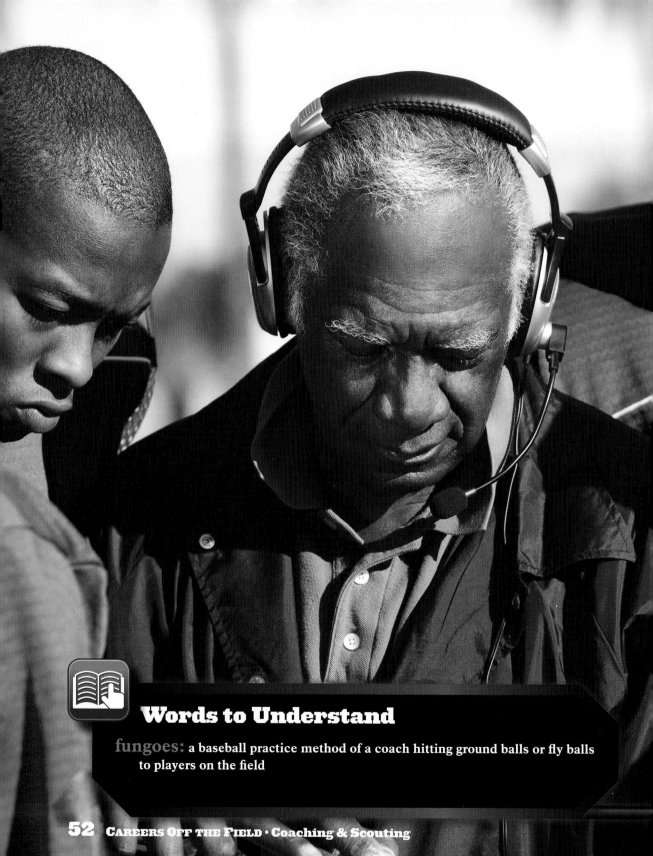

Words to Understand

fungoes: a baseball practice method of a coach hitting ground balls or fly balls to players on the field

The Nitty-Gritty

At almost every level, coaches share a set of key tasks that are common across most sports. Here's a look at how some of these veteran coaches get those jobs done.

Choosing a Team

At most levels, the head coach of a team makes the final decisions about who is on the team. That's a big responsibility, and it comes with pluses and minuses.

On the plus side, coaches get to determine the makeup of their team from the talent available. If they have a particular style of play, they can pick players who match that style. If they are adding players to an existing roster, they can fill in holes that will make the team better. The process of meeting and trying out players is the first step in building the good communication mentioned in Chapter 1.

On the negative side, of course, some players might not make the cut. Telling a player that he or she has not made it is hard. It's hard on the player, hard on the player's parents, and hard on the coach. Whether at the high school or college level, it might mean a coach is the bearer of the news that a lifelong dream is over. At the pro level, there is disappointment, of course. However, there is often a business aspect to organizing a pro team that turns cutting a player from a crushing blow—though it's never easy—into a business decision. Plus, in most cases, pros have options to try other teams. That's not the case with high school or most college situations.

Making sure that all players trying out understand both possibilities—making it or not making it—is crucial for a coach. That's where communication ability comes into play again. A clearly written plan that all players can read and understand will help when the inevitable disappointment happens.

Sometimes, though, the coach has to make a tough call even after the team is assembled and well into a season. Five-time national-champion baseball manager Bill Pintard says, however, that there is addition by subtraction.

"If you have a player—and it doesn't matter how good he is—and he is not fitting into the system, he is a source of disruption. He is not a team player. He puts himself ahead of everybody else. You need to remove him from your team. People gravitate toward good players as leaders, but some of those lead you the wrong way. One season, we got rid of our starting shortstop and second baseman because they were not leading in the right way, and we went on to win the national championship. That would not have happened with those guys in the lineup."

Once the whole team is together, that's when the real fun of coaching begins.

Planning a Practice

For many athletes, practice is their least favorite part of being with a team or playing a sport. For most coaches, practice is where they thrive. Practice is where coaches' passion for teaching and their passion for the sport can have its purest form.

Planning practice strategy in any sport has three main aims: improve players' skills; create and increase a team's togetherness; and get players and team ready for the game. It's also important to remember, as Bill Pintard says, "to use your time wisely. You only have so much time. Once you spend it, it's gone forever."

In terms of teaching, what a practice might include depends a lot on the level of the team. A high school practice might have several sessions aimed at a specific skill, such as dribbling through traffic in the lane in basketball or turning a double play in baseball. Practice, repetition, and instruction are the ways that skills are learned and improved. A college practice, however, might spend more time on tactical and strategic situations. How should a linebacker read an opposing team's offense? What plays should a point guard run in a particular game situation? How can a tennis player read his opponent to find out a weakness to exploit?

In terms of creating togetherness, that comes from positive time spent as a unit. Coaches should praise cooperation and look to avoid splintering the group. Shared hard work, even shared sweaty workouts, are a good way to help a team jell—to come together and work as one unit. Some high school or college coaches take their teams on weekend retreats where they can bond as people as well as teammates. Finally, teaching and togetherness both have to be used in strategic ways to get players ready for their games, both mentally and physically.

Coaches each have their own favorite ways to organize practice. New coaches can look at a wide variety of printed and Internet resources for new ideas on drills, organizing principles, and schedules. Former University of Oregon football coach Chip

Kelly, who moved to the NFL's Philadelphia Eagles in 2013, famously scheduled his Oregon practices down to individual minutes.

High school coaches have an additional challenge: keeping easily bored teenagers engaged. "You have to keep them moving," says the Foresters' Bill Pintard. "The worst part of practice in baseball, for instance, is one guy pitching and one guy hitting, and everyone else shagging. That does not work. You need to

The NFL's Philadelphia Eagles, including quarterback Nick Foles (9), had to learn a new way of practicing when super-organized coach Chip Kelly took over.

make sure everyone is moving, **fungoes** are being hit, a screen lets infielders throw and catch, outfielders need to treat every ball like it's real. It's important that the skipper have a plan and keep things moving."

Coaches at the high school and college levels also have to be very aware of rules in place to limit practice times. Making a mistake by practicing too long, in the wrong ways (such as using pads in football at a time that's not allowed), or practicing out of season can have penalties that can hurt the team. It's more paperwork, but the time spent learning those rules can save headaches later on.

Finally, at the pro level, in many cases coaches say that although the players are prime athletes, they still

A player-turned-coach such as Brooklyn's Jason Kidd (left) can help even stars like Paul Pierce improve their games.

need work on the fine points of their skills. That's particularly true in minor league baseball or hockey, for instance, or the NBA's development leagues. "It's about player development," says former longtime Yankees coach Mickey Kelleher. "It's our job to make sure they achieve at the highest level."

Scouting Work Product

The main work product of a scout is a scouting report. Each sport has its own formats and types of information, but the basics are true for most sports.

"Writing reports is really an art form," says Yankees scout Robby Massar. "You have to be as brief as possible. When I first started I was writing paragraph after paragraph, and it was clearly not right. But I learned that you have to tell the story in just a few words. You learn the key phrases and words that are part of your sport's vocabulary."

"A scouting report on a player fits on one page," said Chicago White Sox scout Gary Woods. "On that one page, you have to write about tools, injuries, makeup, strength, weaknesses, and percentage chance of success. I'm very limited in terms of characters; I have to be very precise, with no fluff. It has to be to the point right away."

In the end, coaching is about relationships—building them and keeping them, often for life.

The Sporting Life

The love of sports and competition draws many former athletes into a life of coaching. People who make that choice can stay part of the sports that they love, but they also have to understand that as leaders, they have different goals and responsibilities. As the experts in this book have shown, coaching is a mental exercise, not the physical activity of the sport itself. Great coaches know their sports inside and out, but they have to know their athletes just as well. The related field of scouting has similar demands on a person: long hours, hard work, and a lot of mental activity.

However, as all these experts also said, people with the right amount of passion can continue to make sports part of their lives.

Text-Dependent Questions

1. According to Bill Pintard, why is high school coaching a bit different than other kinds?

2. What NFL coach was well known for his precise practice schedules?

3. Are scouting reports long or short…and why?

Research Project

Check out fantasy sports. By picking a team of pro players in your favorite sport, you can pretend to be the coach. Study the league rules and choose the team that you think will score the highest. Or join a league with your friends and see who can be the best "head coach" of a fantasy sports team.

Find Out More

Books

Blauner, Andrew. *Coach: 25 Writers Reflect on People Who Made a Difference*. Albany, N.Y.: State University of Albany Press, 2011.

Martens, Rainer. *Successful Coaching*. Champaign, Ill.: Human Kinetics, 2004.

Web Sites

www.coachad.com

The site of the national magazine *Coach and Athletic Director* is packed with articles, advice, interviews, and practice ideas for coaches of just about every sport, mostly at the high school and college level. See the September 2012 issue for a detailed look at an entire high school sports program, including interviews with numerous coaches.

careerplanning.about.com/cs/occupations/p/sports_coach.htm

This site has a quick overview of facts and strategies to look at when considering a coaching career.

Plus, consider looking up the biographies of the coaches featured in this book. Look at their pro team or college athletic department Web sites. See how they took their journeys to their current jobs.

Series Glossary of Key Terms

academic: relating to classes and studies

alumni: people who graduate from a particular college

boilerplate: a standard set of text and information that an organization puts at the end of every press release

compliance: the action of following rules

conferences: groups of schools that play each other frequently in sports

constituencies: a specific group of people related by their connection to an organization or demographic group

credential: a document that gives the holder permission to take part in an event in a way not open to the public

eligibility: a student's ability to compete in sports, based on grades or other school or NCAA requirements

entrepreneurs: people who start their own companies

freelance: a person who does not work full-time for a company, but is paid for each piece of work

gamer: in sports journalism, a write-up of a game

intercollegiate: something that takes places between two schools, such as a sporting event

internships: positions that rarely offer pay but provide on-the-job experience

objective: material written based solely on the facts of a situation

orthopedics: the branch of medicine that specializes in preventing and correcting problems with bones and muscles

recruiting: the process of finding the best athletes to play for a team

revenue: money earned from a business or event

spreadsheets: computer programs that calculate numbers and organize information in rows and columns

subjective: material written from a particular point of view, choosing facts to suit the opinion

Index

Credits

Keith Allison: 34; Dreamstime.com: Luckybusiness 20, RTrembly 24, Libux 77 26,
Kephotos 28, photographerlondon 52, Monkeybusinessimages 60;
Eric Isaacs: 8, 11, 14, 43, 46; Newscom: Chris Williams/ICON Sportswire 16, 32; Cliff
Welch/ICON 22; Will Vragovic/Tampa Bay Times 35; Purnell/ICON 38; Andy Mead/
YCJ/ICON 40; Paul Keeul/ActionPlus 45; UCSB Athletics: 31; USA Basketball: 41;
Gavin Baker/ICON 57; David Santiago/MCT 58.

About the Author

James Buckley Jr. has been a sportswriter and sports media professional for more than 25 years. He was an editor at *Sports Illustrated* and NFL Publishing, was the editor of *NFL Magazine*, and has written more than 100 books on sports for adults and young readers. He also volunteers as the media relations director for the Santa Barbara Foresters, a five-time national champion summer collegiate baseball team.

A special dedication to Chicago White Sox scout Gary Woods, who was such a big help in making this book. Gary passed away just as we were going to press. With this book, we honor him and his passion for helping young athletes.